Quilting with your feet

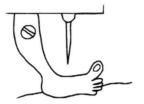

by
Linnette Whicker-Dowdell
and
Kim Fillmore

THIS IS WHERE WE SAY A HUGE
THANK YOU!!!

Linnette & Kim

We spent countless hours shooting picture after picture of each other - and still not one good shot! So...we gave up and decided to have our portrait done by an expert! We found the perfect place - The Portrait Studio - you know...at the mall, $5.00, sit in the booth, close the black curtains and smile!

A special thanks to my husband and best friend, Robert, for his confidence in everything I do, and for his patience and understanding with things left undone while I'm busy pursuing projects like this book.

I also want to thank my good friend and business partner, Kim, for moving to Florida and working with me on this project and many more to come.

Many thanks to all of my family for their support and encouragement.

Linnette

A huge thank you to Daddy, Mom, Lorie, Jodie, Kathy & my very best friend in the whole world - my daughter Elena - for putting up with me "warts and all" and encouraging and supporting no matter what I wanted to pursue. I'm really doing what I truly love.

And what would I do without my friend and business partner, Linnette? Many long distance phone calls of "what if" later, I made it to Florida so we could finally pursue what we'd talked about for so long...writing and creating.

Kim

Between us, we have over 75 years sewing experience (yep, we're that old)! After 23 of those (combined) working directly in the sewing industry...teaching, writing, appearing in videos, tv and magazines, we realized the next logical step was to join our love of sewing together to write and create and share what we've learned.

We wish you endless hours of happy, creative stitching!

TABLE OF CONTENTS

WELCOME to
QUILTING WITH YOUR FEET

So often we talk with machine owners who have purchased one or more of the extra accessory feet available for their sewing machine, and they have commented that they have no idea why they purchased the foot or what to do with it. QUILTING WITH YOUR FEET was written to instruct you in the use of many of the wide array of accessory feet available for your sewing machine. We hope this information will inspire you to use your sewing machine and specialty feet to their fullest capabilities.

As with any sewing, the proper needles, thread, batting and stabilizers will produce the best results. With this in mind, we have included some basic information on the specific products we used to create our quilt to help you select the proper tools to enhance your creativity.

We hope you will use the techniques in the creation of your quilt as a springboard for your own creative ideas. Let your imagination be your guide as you create your own one of a kind originals.

It is always best to purchase the machine parts and accessories designed specifically for your machine - these are the feet & accessories that will produce the best results on your particular machine model. However, if your machine does not have a sewing foot of the type described, you may be able to utilize a generic or different brand foot - with or without the use of an adapter shank.

If you attempt to use another brand foot, you'll need to test to make sure the needle hole in the foot aligns properly with the needle hole in the plate of your machine.

Although standard low shank feet can be used with adapters on most machines, you may find the quality of your results are not as precise as with a foot manufactured specifically for your machine/model.

Availability of an adapter does NOT mean you will be able to successfully use every foot on the market...it means you have the opportunity to try to use another foot on your machine...again...the results may not be as precise as a foot manufactured specifically for your model.

You will need to determine if you need an adapter to use these other feet. Machine feet come in 5 basic types, while most accessory feet at this time are standard low-shank. Determine what type feet your machine uses. If the shank and needle opening of the accessory foot you are interested in match what your machine uses, there's a pretty good chance the foot will work with your machine. If the accessory doesn't match, i.e. different shank, needle hole doesn't match your machine, different type of snap-on - you'll need to look for an adapter or a different style of foot:

- Low Shank - approx. 1/2" from bottom of foot to center of attaching screw.
- High Shank - approx. 1" from bottom of foot to center of attaching screw
- Slant Needle - (found on older model Singer machines) - shank is at a slight angle to the foot - approx. 1" from bottom of foot to center of attaching

screw
- Extra High Shank - (found on older model Kenmore machines) - shank is a bit higher than a standard high shank - high shank feet WILL NOT work, but an adapter is available to allow use of standard low-shank feet.
- Bernina - no attaching screw - feet attach by pulling a lever over the protrusion on the side of the foot. Bernina DOES have an adapter shank that allows use of standard low-shank feet.

FUN FEET

NOTE: Your presser feet may NOT look exactly like those pictured.

1/4" Quilting Foot

With or without edge guide. Use this foot for joining fabric pieces. Clearance between the needle and the outer edge of the foot is 1/4" ; some 1/4" piecing feet also have a marking for 1/8" seams as used for mini-quilt piecing.

Bias Binder

Various types are available. Use this foot to apply bias binding to light and medium-weight fabrics.

Circular Embroidery Guide*

Use this foot for embroidering perfect circular motifs using decorative threads and stitches. *See Circle Secrets and Other Slick Tips (beginning on page 15) for alternative methods of embroidering perfect circles.

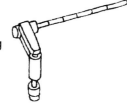

Cording Blade*

Raises the fabric before stitching, to produce more well-defined pintucks. *See Circle Secrets and Other Slick Tips (beginning on page 15) for alternative methods of creating perfect pintucks.

Couching/Braiding Foot

This foot has a large loop or opening that allows heavier braids & cords to be fed under the presser foot. The cord needs to pass smoothly through the loop/opening for the foot to function properly.

Eyelet Plate

This plate covers the feed dogs and has a post in the center allowing you to stitch uniformly around a small cutout hole. Use the eyelet plate to embroider belt eyelets or decorative flowered eyelets.

FUN FEET (continued)

Fagoting/Bridging Guides

A simple tool that creates a uniform space between 2 finished fabric edges. Use this guide for sewing together two edges of fabric or ribbons with a hem-stitch effect. *See Circle Secrets and Other Slick Tricks (beginning on page 15) for alternative methods of fagoting.

Free-Motion Quilting Foot/Darning Foot

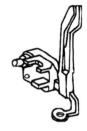

A round or square foot that holds the fabric taut against the needle plate on the downswing of the needle. The foot raises as the needle raises to allow the fabric to be moved. The larger free-motion quilting foot has markings that are typically used to maintain an even distance from a seamline.

Fringe Sewing Foot

A foot with a tall guide in the center that forces the thread to build-up in loops. This foot can be used to sew fringes, tailor tacks, fringed flowers and fagoting.

Gathering/Shirring Foot

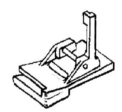

A metal or plastic foot with a double-layer guide on the front. Typically the fabric to be gathered goes under the foot, while the fabric you are attaching to feeds through the upper guide. Tightening the upper tension can produce fuller gathering. Recommended for lighter-weight fabrics.

Multi-Hole Cord Foot

A foot with multiple small holes or guides that allow cords to feed evenly spaced under the presser foot. Couch cords using decorative or construction stitches and your favorite embroidery or monofilament thread.

Narrow Edge/Edge Joining Foot

A foot with a flat blade positioned vertically in the center. This foot allows you to easily align two fabric or ribbon edges together for joining (such as fabric to lace), evenly spacing topstitching rows, creating perfectly joined laces, stitch-in-the-ditch quilting.

FUN FEET (continued)

Open Toe Applique' Foot

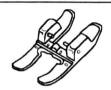

The open front of this foot allows for a full view of the stitching area.

Pintuck Foot

Pintuck feet have from 3 to 9 small grooves on the bottom. Pintuck feet are used with a twin needle to create small tucks (folds) on light to medium weight fabric. Check with your foot manufacturer for guidance on the size of twin needle to use with your particular foot. Generally a size 1.6 to 2.5mm width twin needle is appropriate.

Pintuck Foot with Guide

Similar to a standard pintuck foot, but has an attached guide on the side that creates a uniform space for adding decorative stitches in between tucks. Use this foot to create spaced pintucks and to guide decorative stitching between the tucks.

Piping/Cording/Knit Edge Foot

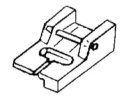

A plastic or metal foot with a fairly deep tunnel under the center. This allows the foot to easily feed over heavier cords, multiple cords or pre-strung pearls to create piping or decorative couched effects. The foot can also be used for gathering single layer lighter-weight fabrics by lengthing the stitch length and tightening the upper thread tension.

Rolled Hem Foot

Available in various finished widths. Use this foot to stitch perfect double-folded rolled hems.

Straight Stitch Needle Plate

A straight stitch needle plate is perfect for any straight stitch work - topstitching, quilting, heirloom. It can be used with straight stitch in center needle position only. The straight stitch plate is especially useful when joining quilt pieces and keeps the fabric from being pushed through the wider opening of a standard needle plate.

NEEDLE NOTES

What type & size needle should I use?

If it seems like there are different types of needles for every type of sewing...well, there are! Is there a law that says if you're quilting, you must use a quilting needle? No...the needle police have never shown up at our houses! However, specialty needles have been created for a reason and often mean the difference between a so-so quality project and a perfect project. For instance, the quilting needle has been designed to eliminate "bearding" on your quilts - those little bits of batting fuzz that can pull through to the top surface of your quilt. And...Topstitch needles were designed with a larger needle eye to allow heavier-weight threads to pass smoothly through the eye. We've included basic information about the needles used for the projects in this book.

What about needle size? As a rule, the finer the fabric, the finer the needle. However, when embellishing fabric, this rule can be thrown out the window! Don't be afraid to experiment - heavy thread on fine fabric, lightweight thread on heavy fabric and leather...and just match the needle to the thread weight.

To choose the right needle size, let the weight of the thread be your first guide. Make sure the thread passes smoothly through the needle eye with no dragging. If the thread drags, you'll likely end up with shredding and breaking and lots of frustration! For instance, 12-weight cotton thread generally feeds more smoothly through a size 90 or 100 topstitch needle than through a Universal needle of the same size.

Your second guide is the type of fabric and technique being used. Sewing on heavy fabric doesn't necessarily mean you must use a big, giant, fat needle! Generally a size 90 or 100 needle will pierce most fabrics - using a larger needle will only produce bigger holes in your fabric! If that's the look you're going for - then use the larger needle! Don't be afraid to experiment with different needle sizes and techniques. You'll find your own favorite combinations that work best for your projects and machine.

Change the needle to suit the weight of the thread and have fun with embellishing. It is meant as a creative outlet...sewing "outside the box"!

When should I change the needle?

General rule of thumb...new project = new needle. While you may be able to continue using a needle that was used on a previous project, the cost of a single needle is quite inexpensive compared to replacing fabric that's been ruined. There are, however, other indications that it's time to change the needle - if you learn to watch for the signals:

NEEDLE NOTES (continued)

- The most obvious signal is, of course, if your needle breaks! And we've all been through that one! Just make sure when you replace the broken needle, you look for the broken pieces and remove them from the machine. These little bits of broken needle can cause major damage if they become lodged in the bobbin area of your machine.

- Shredding and breaking thread generally means that the eye of the needle has become sharp - and will just continue to get worse if you continue trying to use the same needle. Thread passing through the eye of the needle actually sharpens the eye - just like a knife on a sharpening stone!

- A "thumping" sound that wasn't there when you started sewing with a new needle? The point of a sewing machine needle will become dull through normal use. "Listen" to the sound your machine makes when you use a new needle, you'll soon learn to notice a difference in the sound. This is an indication the needle needs to be replaced.

- Snags and pulls in your fabric generally mean there is a burr or rough spot on the needle and it is catching the fibers as the needle pierces the fabric.

Also keep in mind, fabrics made of synthetic fibers will dull needles more quickly than fabrics made of natural fibers. If a needle is slightly damaged or has a burr, it can cause pulled threads, damaging the fabric's weave. It can also cause the thread to break while sewing. Simply changing to a new needle can cure a LOT of ills when it comes to perfect projects!

NEEDLE NOTES (continued)

Embroidery	The eye of the Embroidery needle is elongated for use with heavier decorative threads as well as a deeper front groove on the needle to help eliminate shredding and skipping.
Universal	A Universal needle has a point halfway between a true sharp and a ballpoint and will sew equally well on most woven and some knit fabrics.
Topstitch	Slight ball point with an elongated eye for topstitching with heavy threads. The needle you'll want to use with all your topstitching weight threads.
Twin	The first size number indicates the distance between the two needle points in millimeters; the second number indicates the size of the needles. Twin needles are used to sew two parallel rows of decorative stitching or with a straight stitch to create pintucks.

IMPORTANT!! Do not attempt to use twin needles that are wider than the needle plate opening of your machine. This will only break needles and damage your needle plate.

Don't be afraid to try decorative stitching with twin needles! Just remember to narrow the pattern width to accommodate the needle width. Simply subtract the width of the needle from the widest stitch your machine will sew. The resulting number is the widest width you can stitch the pattern. For example, you are using a 2.0mm twin needle and the widest stitch your machine can sew is 6.0mm. Simply subtract 2.0mm from 6.0mm to determine that the widest stitch you can sew is 4.0mm! Simple! And you'll discover some wonderful new stitches you didn't know your machine could do!

Some machines also have the ability to "tell" the machine what width twin needle you are using! If you have this capability, follow your particular machine instructions for this feature.

Quilting	Specifically designed to make quilting by machine even easier. The specially designed point helps eliminate bearding on your quilt projects...those little fuzzy bits of batting that can poke through to the top of your quilt when using a standard needle.

THREADS

Current-day sewing & embroidery machines are manufactured to handle a wide variety of thread types and weights, and thread options are definitely varied and plentiful for the home sewing enthusiast! The key to selecting threads is simple...if you have little exposure to the thread market, it is best to initially sew with name-brand threads and threads recommended by your sewing machine dealer. Typically your machine dealer will carry one or more brands of threads. This is a good place to start, but from there the sky's the limit! Don't be afraid to experiment with new and interesting threads. Your machine dealer should be able to guide you as to what threads can be used on your particular machine model. With the proper needle size and type you can make your wildest embellishing ideas come to life!

The thread and needle combinations we used for this quilt are recommendations only. You may find that you prefer a completely different combination of needle/thread than what is suggested, or that your machine runs better using different combinations. Again...don't be afraid to experiment. We promise the sewing, quilting, embroidery police will NEVER show up on your doorstep!

THREAD WEIGHT: The guideline here is the **lower** the number, the **heavier** the thread! For instance, a No. 30 thread is heavier than a No. 40 -- this is helpful to know if you have an embroidery pattern that doesn't fill as densely as you would like with 40 weight thread...simply substitute a 30 weight thread and notice the difference in the appearance.

The thread weight and type will help determine the size and type of needle you will need to use to obtain the best results.

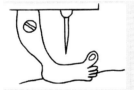

Make sure you DO NOT attempt to use hand quilting thread on your machine. Hand quilting threads are generally waxed (or have another similar finish) and can gum up your machine.

Most of the thread types we've listed are available from a variety of manufacturers. There are a couple of the threads we've used that are brand specific. On these brand specific threads, we've also listed the manufacturer.

Bobbins

Prewound bobbins are always a convenience, but not always available in the color you may need. The variety and brand of bobbin threads available for winding yourself are numerous - and available in either a polyester or cotton fiber.

100% cotton bobbin threads tend to be more forgiving, producing less puckering of your

THREADS (cont.)

fabric. Cotton thread stretches a bit while sewing/embroidering to fit the length of the stitch being sewn. It will retain this longer length after your stitching is complete, causing less puckering of your fabric.

Polyester threads (either pre-wound or on a spool) are great where strength is an issue, such as outdoor projects that are affected by the sun, but are much less forgiving when it comes to puckering of your fabric/embroideries. Polyester threads start out in a liquid form and have a permanent "memory" built right in. This means that the thread can stretch while embroidering/sewing due to the heat caused by the speed of the machine. Your stitching may look just beautiful as soon as you remove it from the machine, but puckering can appear as the thread cools and returns to it's original shape/length.

It's important that you determine what bobbin thread works best with your machine and for your projects.

Cotton Quilting Thread	Machine quilting thread is made from long staple cotton fibers. "Long staple fiber" means that the thread will produce almost no fuzz or lint.
Cotton Embroidery Thread	A 100% cotton thread that is perfect for machine and hand embroidery, lacemaking, crocheting, tatting, quilting. Cotton embroidery thread produces a more "vintage" look to your embroidery.
Monofilament	A clear or smoke-colored thread, monofilament is most often used for machine quilting, couching decorative threads and topstitching...anywhere you want the thread to be "invisible". If you find it necessary to use monofilament in the bobbin, make sure you only wind the bobbin half full and at a slow speed. Monofilament thread heats and stretches excessively if wound at a high speed and as it cools can actually bend or break your bobbin. If you've ever had this happen, you know just what we mean!

THREADS (cont.)

Pearl Crown Rayon

A YLI brand thread. A versatile heavy-weight rayon embroidery cord. Similar in weight to pearl cotton. This thread does not run through a needle eye, but is wonderful for bobbin work - wind a bobbin and sew/embroider from the wrong side of your project, or use for couching techniques.

Rayon Embroidery Thread

Rayon embroidery threads are readily available in 2 weights - 30 or 40. 40-Weight is the most commonly found and used for most general embroidery. 30-Weight is great for those embroidery designs that are less-densely filled in than you'd like. The slightly heavier 30-weight thread fills in the gaps a little more fully than a 40-weight thread. 30-weight rayon threads generally provide better coverage on napped fabrics such as velour and terrycloth.

Standard Sewing Thread

Standard sewing threads typically come in three types: 100% polyester, cotton-wrapped polyester and 100% mercerized cotton. A good rule of thumb is to match fibre content, i.e. cotton fabric/cotton thread, poly fabric/poly or poly/blend thread. Because of its stability, cotton thread tends to produce fewer puckers in your seams.

12-Weight Cotton

A Sulky brand thread. This 12-weight, 2-ply twisted, long staple 100% Egyptian cotton embroidery thread produces a very heavy fill-in effect that looks like crewel embroidery.

STABILIZERS

Stabilizers...a type for every project! We all wish there was just one stabilizer that would work for every project, but this just isn't possible. No one stabilizer is perfect for every project or fabric type. So...we've included basic information about the three types we used for this project.

Typing paper, old computer paper, coffee filters and toilet paper are NOT stabilizers! Sewing/Embroidery stabilizers have been manufactured specifically for use on machines. They generate very little residue, while allowing removal of as much of the stabilizer as possible.

Always test-embroider on a scrap of your project fabric backed with your chosen stabilizer prior to stitching. The extra time spent stitching out a sample is well worth the end-result.

TEAR-AWAY	Medium weight stabilizers ideal for all types of embroidery and decorative stitching. Tear away from around embroidery after stitching is completed. Stabilizer will remain under stitched areas.
WATER SOLUBLE (available in both paper and plastic types)	Hot, warm and cold-water soluble are all available. A single layer of heavyweight is generally enough for embroidering delicate, sheer fabric and lace. Single or multiple layers may be used as required. A single layer of a lightweight works well as a topper for embroidering towels and other napped items. Water solubles can also be used as a template to stitch through for transferring designs onto fabric. By dissolving a piece of the soluble in water, a liquid stabilizer is formed which can be brushed on sheer and flimsy fabric for body before stitching.
LIQUID	Liquid stabilizers are especially good when every bit of stabilizer must be removed from a project after stitching. Available as a spray or brush-on. All of the stabilizer can be washed out of the project when embroidery is complete.

QUILT BATTING

Cotton, polyester/cotton, polyester, wool and silk...the fiber choice is really a personal choice. We used low loft bonded fiber polyester batting. The advantage of a bonded batting is that the light resin coating adds strength, helps to prevent fiber migration (bearding) and does not require extensive quilting. When cutting the batting for your quilt, it is advisable to add 4" all the way around for a full size quilt and 2" all the way around for a wall hanging or baby quilt to allow for the batting that will be drawn up while quilting. This extra batting will be trimmed away when the quilting is complete and you are ready to square up the quilt and add the binding.

CIRCLE SECRETS & OTHER SLICK TIPS!

While we strongly recommend that you always use the accessories designed for your specific machine, we know that sometimes there are accessories that are not available for all models. We have a few solutions we hope you'll find useful. These tips utilize common household items...small coffee stir straws, round toothpicks, thumbtacks and embroidery hoops!

Look around your house...you may just come up with your own "household" sewing aid!

Thumbtack Circles

- Size 80/12 Universal or Embroidery Needle
- Flat Head Thumbtack
- Open Toe Applique' Foot
- Duct Tape or Heavy Cloth Tape
- Light to Medium Weight Woven Fabric
- Stabilizer
- Rayon Embroidery Threads

If a circle guide is not available for your machine, you can use a flat-backed thumbtack to make perfect circles of any size using built-in decorative stitches!

1. To create your Thumbtack Circle Guide, poke a thumbtack through a piece of duct tape or heavy fabric tape - the head of the thumbtack should be on the adhesive side of the tape so the point of the tack is poking through from the non-adhesive side. To use the guide, determine how big a circle you want to stitch, divide this number in half and position the point of the tack this distance directly to the left of the needle. For example, if you want to create a 5" circle, position the tack 2 ½" directly to the left of the needle. Press the tape securely down to the bed of your machine.

2. Attach the foot and thread the machine with rayon embroidery thread. Mark a dot on the fabric where you want the exact center of the circle. Place a layer of stabilizer under your fabric. Push the fabric and stabilizer onto the thumbtack at the marked dot. Select the stitch of your choice and sew your first circle. Don't make yourself nuts trying to guide the fabric...the fabric will guide itself! All you need to do is make sure that the thumbtack stays in place!

3. Reposition the tack closer or farther from the needle to create another circle inside or outside of the originally stitched circle. Continue in this manner until you've stitched the desired number of circles. Just remember, the distance the tack is placed from the needle is 1/2 the width of the finished circle!

Embroidery Hoop Circles

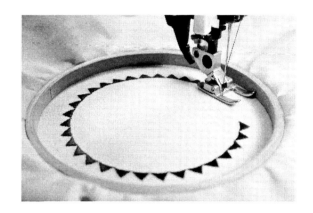

- Size 80/12 Universal or Embroidery Needle
- Machine Embroidery Hoops of Various Sizes
- Open Toe Applique' Foot
- Light to Medium Weight Woven Fabric
- Stabilizer
- Rayon Embroidery Threads

A simple way to embroider perfect circles using embroidery hoops!

While any embroidery hoops will work, machine embroidery hoops are thinner, making it easier to slide under your presser foot!

1. Attach the presser foot and thread the machine with rayon embroidery thread. Place a piece of stabilizer under the fabric to be embroidered. Hoop the fabric and stabilizer.

2. Position the hooped fabric under the foot with the edge of the hoop riding next to the foot. Keeping the majority of the hoop to the left of the needle allows you to use any size round hoop.

3. Select the desired decorative stitch and sew around the circle keeping the hoop next to the foot. Repeat the process using different size embroidery hoops to create different size circles!

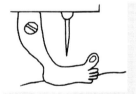

If you have a computerized machine with adjustable pattern length, it's easy to make the patterns meet perfectly. About 2 inches from where the stitches will meet, measure the remaining space. Measure the exact length of one repeat. Divide this number into the remaining length to determine how many motifs will fit. Adjust the length of the stitch to fit exactly in the space. For example, if you have 40mm of remaining space and are sewing 12mm patterns, 12 does not divide evenly into 40, but 10 does! Simply adjust your pattern to 10mm in length and sew the remaining 4 motifs! You may have to readjust the final motif. If you do not have a computerized machine, it is still possible to make the stitches meet. "Manipulate" the fabric by gently holding the fabric back or helping the fabric along to make the stitch design meet at the end of your circle.

Toothpick Pintucks

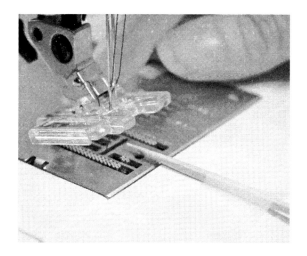

- 2.0/80 Twin Needle
- Pintuck Foot or Pintuck Foot with Guide
- Round Toothpick
- Soft Cotton Fabric
- Spray Stabilizer (lightly stabilize fabric before stitching)
- 2 spools standard sewing thread

If a cording blade is not available for your machine, a round toothpick works just great to raise the fabric producing well-defined, crisp pintucks!

1. Insert the twin needle in your machine and thread with desired thread. Attach foot.

2. Tape a round toothpick to the bed of the sewing machine centered between the two needles, making sure the tip of the toothpick DOES NOT sit within the needle plate opening.

3. Sew the pintucks. As you sew, the fabric will be raised slightly as it rides over the toothpick, producing a more well-defined pintuck.

Coffee Stir Straw Corded Pintucks

A coffee stir straw is just the thing for guiding cord to create beautiful corded pintucks. Keep in mind - stir STICKS won't work - no hole for the cord to go through!

- Size 2.0/80 Twin Needle
- Pintuck Foot or Pintuck Foot with Guide
- Gimp Cord
- Plastic Coffee Stir Straw
- Lightweight Woven Fabric
- Spray Stabilizer (lightly stabilize fabric before stitching)

1. Insert the twin needle into the machine and thread with desired thread. Attach foot.

2. Cut a 1" piece of the coffee stirrer.

3. Tape the 1" coffee stirrer to the bed of the sewing machine so it sits in front of the presser foot and is centered between the two needles.

4. Thread the gimp cord through the hole in the coffee stirrer.

5. Sew the pintucks, making sure that the gimp cord in secured in the pintuck as you sew.

Coffee Stir Straw Bridging Guide

Creating a bridging guide is as simple as connecting two 1" lengths of small coffee stir straws together!

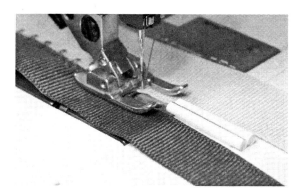

- Small Coffee Stir Straw
- Open Toe Applique' Foot
- Lightweight Woven Fabrics or Ribbons To Be Joined
- 12 Weight Cotton Thread
- Size 100 Topstitch Needle
- Clear Tape

1. If joining fabric, clean finish the raw edges to be joined.

2. Insert the topstitching needle.

3. Thread the machine with the 12 weight cotton thread. Select a bridging stitch such as a feather stitch.

4. Tape 2 - 1" sections of stir straw together. Tape these to the bed of the sewing machine centered in front of the needle and presser foot.

5. Position one finished fabric edge or ribbon on each side of the coffee stir straws and sew, taking care to keep the fabrics butted up next to the stir straws.

6. As you sew, the stitch should just catch the edge of the fabric or ribbon on both pieces leaving a space in the center. Adjust your stitch width as needed.

Continuous Bias

A little fabric goes a long way when making bias. A 36" square will yield approximately 13 yards of 2½" wide bias. An 18" square will create plenty of bias for our quilt.

- Size 80/12 Universal needle
- Standard sewing foot
- Sewing thread
- 18" Square Cotton Fabric to match quilt
- Fabric Marker
- Rotary Cutter, Mat & Ruler or Scissors

1. Cut an 18" square from your selected binding fabric.

2. Cut the square in half diagonally to create two triangles.

3. With right sides together, sew the straight grain edges together with a ¼" seam to form a parallelogram. Press the seam open.

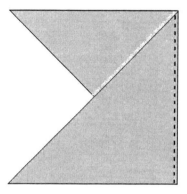

4. Mark the fabric with a line parallel to the bias at the desired width. Continue marking lines across the entire piece of fabric. Depending on the width of your strips, you may have fewer or more strips and a small unused section at one edge.

5. Number the marked sections starting with "0" on one edge of the fabric and starting with "1" on the opposite edge of the fabric.

6. Ignore the 0 line.

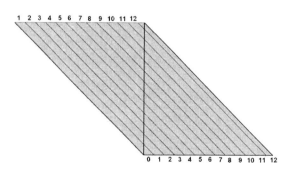

7. Line up the numbered rows starting with 1 to create an offset in the fabric tube. Sew together with a ¼" seam. While you are stitching the seam, the fabric will be bunched and look like it couldn't possibly lay smooth. Never fear...once you've completed the seam, the tube will miraculously smooth itself out!

8. Starting at the offset end, use the rotary cutter, mat & ruler to cut around the tube on the marked lines to create the continuous bias.

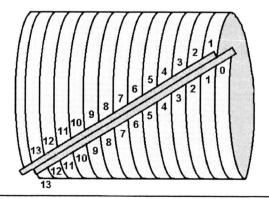

Free-Motion or Stipple Quilting

Stippling is a free motion quilting technique often used to fill in background areas. You are in control of the stitching. With the feed dogs dropped, you determine the stitch length by moving the fabric.

- Size 80/12 Quilting needle
- Monofilament thread
- Free Motion Quilting Foot or Darning Foot
- Basted quilt
- Straight Stitch Needle Plate

1. Insert Quilting needle. Change to Straight Stitch Needle Plate. Thread the machine with the monofilament thread. Select the straight stitch.

2. Attach the Free Motion Quilting foot or Darning Foot. The free-motion foot or darning foot holds the fabric while the stitch is being formed and releases the fabric when the stitch has been completed allowing you to easily move the fabric as you sew. You are in control of the stitching. The stitch length is determined by how fast or slow you move the fabric.

3. Lower the feed dogs. If you cannot lower the feed dogs on your machine, you may be able to cover them with a special plate for this purpose. If a cover is not available, change the stitch length to zero. This keeps the feed dogs from moving forward and back and catching on the fabric as you stipple.

4. Position the quilt under the presser foot. Sit squarely in front of the machine with your hands positioned on either side of the needle (at 3 and 9 o'clock). There are several products designed to make holding your fabric easier as you sew. Check with your dealer or local quilt shop for availability and recommendations. Adjust your chair height so as your hands are on the quilt, your shoulders are relaxed and your forearms are at a slight angle above the bed of the machine. This allows your arms complete range of motion and keeps your neck and shoulders from becoming overly tired. If you find you're scrunching your shoulders or slouching at your machine...readjust your chair height.

5. Starting at one edge or corner, bring the bobbin thread to the top of the quilt to prevent it from being caught in the stippling. Sew a few stitches in place to secure. Clip the thread tails.

6. Before you begin to stipple, you may want to make a mental plan of your path. You may even want to run your finger over the planned path to set it in your mind...think of where you want to start and end your stippling. If you preplan, you should be able to complete all four tri-

angles of each block without stopping to clip threads. Don't worry if you do not follow that mental plan exactly as you sew. Who's going to know besides you...and anyone you confess to??!

7. When you stipple, move the fabric side to side or forward and back, do not turn the fabric as you stipple. Stippling is usually done with curved lines meandering across the fabric without crossing or touching. It can be as close together as every ½" or as far apart as 2" to 3". This is strictly personal choice and dependant on the desired finished look. Moving the fabric quickly results in longer stitches and moving the fabric slowly results in shorter stitches. Contrary to what you may be inclined to do, the faster you sew, the more in control you will be.

8. If you have never stipple quilted before, practice on scraps first. Just remember to relax. Use the needle down feature when you need to stop to hold the fabric in place so there won't be any long jump stitches when you start stippling again. If you find yourself getting tense or feel tightness in your shoulders, stop and relax or stop and have a cuppa....

9. To secure the threads at the end, sew a few stitches in place and clip the thread tails on the front and the back of the quilt.

Stitch In The Ditch

Stitch in the ditch is a technique in which you simply sew in the seam line. This is an easy technique which makes it a good way to break into quilting. If you use monofilament thread, the stitching will be virtually invisible on the top side of the quilt.

- Edge Joining/Narrow Edge Foot
- Monofilament Thread
- Quilting Needle

1. Thread machine with monofilament thread and insert quilting needle.
2. Start in the center of the quilt. Position foot with center guide riding in the seamline. Sew all of the long straight seams first followed by the diagonal seamlines.

Using a narrow edge foot with a center guide helps to push the fabric down in front of the stitching to help "bury" the stitching in the seam line. If you do not have an Edge Joining/Narrow Edge foot, you will need to carefully guide the quilt so the stitching falls in the "ditch" of the seamlines.

SUPPLIES & MACHINE SETUP

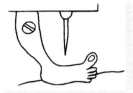 All of the feet, needle, thread and stabilizer types used to complete our Spring Garden quilt are listed beginning on page 5. In <u>this</u> section are the basic machine setup and general fabric requirements for the complete quilt. Each block chapter has a list of individual supplies that are required specifically for that block as well as fabric cutting instructions.

Decorative cords, miscellaneous notions and thread colors are listed with the individual quilt blocks.

Machine Setup

Make sure your sewing/embroidery machine is in good working order. Keep your machine fuzz-free...most machines include a little brush for this purpose. If your machine didn't include a dusting brush, make sure to get one from your dealer. This is one of the most important tools you can have for keeping your machine running in top condition.

While some machines require no oiling (check with your manufacturer), for those that do...clean the fuzz out of the bobbin/hook area and oil the sewing machine as recommended by your manufacturer. A general rule of thumb is every 10 to 15 hours of actual use.

Now, let's get started on creating the blocks for your quilt! Insert a size 80/12 Universal needle, select a straight stitch and set the stitch length at 2.5mm. Read the instructions for each block carefully before beginning, as specialty needles are recommended for some blocks.

Fabric

Select good quality 100% cotton fabrics for your quilt. Cotton quilting fabrics come in every color and pattern of the rainbow and are easier to work with for quilts than synthetics and blends. Cottons are very forgiving fabrics...allowing you to "fudge" here and there, while synthetics and blends have a "memory" that will always return them to their original shape and size...no "fudging" allowed! Specialty fabrics, such as lame' may also be used for special effects but should be backed with a fusible knit interfacing for stability.

Yardage requirements given in this book are based on 40" of usable width to allow for preshrinking and removing selvages. You may have small leftovers...perfect for future projects...or just keeping your fabric shelves warm (like most of us)!

Fabrics You'll Need

- 1/2 yard each of red & yellow 100% cotton fabric
- 5/8 yard green 100% cotton fabric
- 1 yard blue 100% cotton fabric
- 3 yards - 45" wide 100% cotton background fabric (we used off-white)
- 3 yards - 45" wide 100% cotton backing fabric (1 1/2 yds if fabric is 60" or wider)
- 56" x 56" Cotton quilt batting
- 100% cotton sewing thread for quilt construction. If most of your quilt is dark, select a dark gray thread. If most of your quilt is light, select a cream or light gray thread.

Basic Sewing Supplies
(individual supplies for each block
are listed with the block instructions)

- Scissors
- Straight pins
- Safety pins
- Water-soluble fabric marker
- Steam iron
- Rotary cutter
- Rotary cutting mat
- Rotary ruler at least 6" x 12". Your ruler should have 45 degree markings.

Cutting & Stabilizing Instructions for Background Blocks
(all other cutting instructions are listed with the individual blocks)

1. From background fabric, cut 7 - 10" x 10" squares and 2 - 12" x 12" squares.

2. Spray 10" x 10" squares with spray stabilizer. Allow to air dry slightly and press dry. Repeat process until squares are fairly firm. Set aside.

3. Lightly spray 12" x 12" squares with spray stabilizer (for pintuck squares). Allow to air dry slightly and press dry. Set aside. We've found in testing that the fabric tends to feed more smoothly with a slight amount of stabilization.

GARDEN PATH

Supplies You'll Need

- Fringe Sewing Foot
- Eyelet Plate
- Narrow Edge/Edge Joining Foot
- Standard Sewing Foot
- 10" x 10" background fabric
- Size 80/12 Universal or Embroidery needle
- Rayon embroidery thread
- Bobbin
- 1¼ yard 1" wide green grosgrain ribbon
- Wash-away stabilizer
- 5" spring embroidery hoop
- Small sharp scissors
- Tweezers

 If an eyelet plate is not available for your machine, simply substitute your favorite decorative stitches to embellish the ribbons (ill. 1).

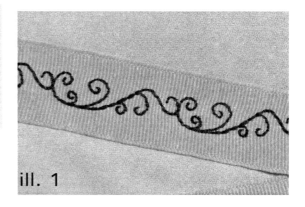

ill. 1

1. Attach the eyelet plate to your machine. Insert the needle and thread with rayon embroidery thread. Insert the bobbin.

2. Cut the grosgrain ribbon into 8" strips.

3. Mark dots on the ribbon wherever you want a fuzzy eyelet to be placed.

4. Separate the rings of the spring embroidery hoop and place the wash-away stabilizer over the outside ring. Lay 2-3 pieces of the grosgrain ribbon on the stabilizer, making sure to posi-

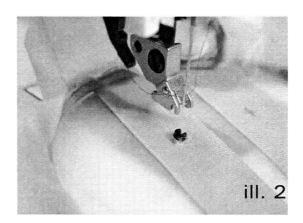

ill. 2

tion so as many of the eyelet marking points are in the hoop as possible. Place the inside ring into the larger outside ring making sure to catch the ends of the ribbon as well as the stabilizer in the hoop. It is important to make sure the stabilizer and ribbon are taut to create successful eyelets (ill. 2).

5. With small sharp scissors, cut a very small hole through the grosgrain ribbon and stabilizer. Push them over the pin on the eyelet plate. They must fit tightly around the pin (ill. 2).

6. Select the zigzag stitch. Change the width to the widest possible setting. Set your machine for free motion embroidery.

7. Sew by pivoting the hoop in a slow even motion around the center hole to produce a smooth satin-stitch all around the snipped hole.

8. Select the zigzag stitch that has a left or right needle position and set for left needle position (you may need to mirror image the stitch).

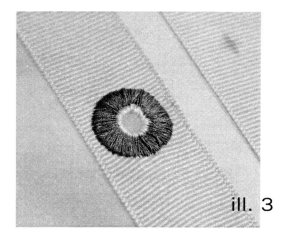

ill. 3

9. Stitch slowly and evenly around the eyelet so that the inner edge of all of the previously sewn stitches are secure. To secure the threads, select the straight stitch and sew a few stitches in place. If necessary, move the needle position to do this (ill. 3).

10. Remove the hoop from the machine, but no not remove the fabric from the hoop.

11. From the wrong side, cut the bobbin thread using small sharp scissors. Turn over to the right side and gently pull the rayon thread to the top. Tweezers work well for this. Place sev-

eral "fuzzy" flowers on each strip of grosgrain ribbon. Create as many "fuzzy flower" strips as you desire to decorate your block. Carefully remove the grosgrain strips from the stabilizer.

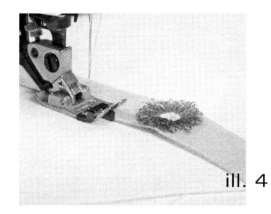

ill. 4

12. Place tear-away or wash-away stabilizer under the background fabric. Position the ribbons on the background block in a pleasing pattern. Cut the ribbon strips to the necessary size to fit the block. Pin in place.

13. Attach the edge joining/narrow edge foot and thread the machine with rayon embroidery thread.

14. Select straight stitch and stitch along both outside edges of each ribbon to hold them in place (ill. 4).

15. Attach the fringe foot to the machine. Select the zigzag stitch. Set the stitch length for a satin stitch and change the width to as wide as your presser foot will allow.

ill.5

16. Position the foot on the right side of the ribbon so that the left swing of the needle just pierces the ribbon and the right swing of the needle is in the background fabric. Be sure to tie off at the beginning and end of the stitching. Sew down the entire edge of the ribbon (ill. 5).

17. Push the loops of fringe to the side and tape in place to keep out of the way while you're stitching in the next step.

ill. 6

18. Attach the standard sewing foot. With the zigzag stitch still selected, change to a 2mm satin stitch setting. Sew along the edge of the ribbon catching the edge of the fringe to secure in place (ill. 6).

19. Turn the fabric over and cut the bobbin thread across each row of fringe. Use tweezers to pull the threads to the top to create "fringe" (ill. 7).

20. Trim block to 7 1/2" square and set aside.

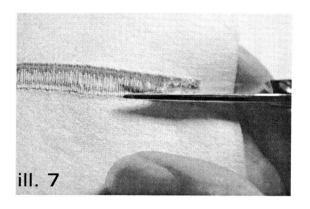

ill. 7

SUNBURST

Supplies You'll Need

- Standard Sewing Foot
- Multi-hole Cording Foot
- Open Toe Applique' Foot
- 10" x 10" background fabric
- Size 12/80 Universal or Embroidery needle
- 4-9 colors of YLI Pearl Crown Rayon threads - 1 cord for each hole/slot of your cording foot.
- Rayon embroidery thread
- Bobbin
- Sullivan's Spray Stabilizer
- Water-soluble fabric marker
- Circle template from pattern section

1. With a fabric marker, draw diagonal, horizontal and vertical lines on the fabric intersecting at the center of the block. Using the template in the pattern section, draw a circle in the center of the fabric square. (ill. 1).

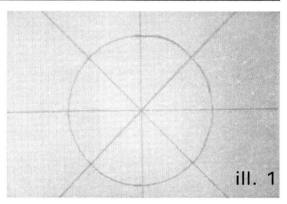

ill. 1

2. Cut 1 1/2 yard lengths of Pearl Crown Rayon thread. We used a multi-hole cording foot with 9 cords (4 repeating colors - yellow, red, green, blue, yellow, blue, green, red, yellow).

Line up the cords in the order you want to insert them in the foot and tape the ends together to your work surface. This will help keep the cords in order and make it easier to thread the foot (ill. 2).

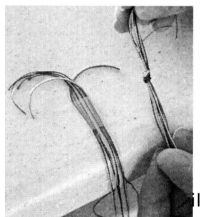

ill. 2

3. Tie a knot in the end of the group of cords to hold them together and keep the cords from slipping out of the foot (ill. 2). Thread the holes/guides of your foot so that the knot is on the bottom side of the foot (ill. 3). For feet that have holes instead of guides, try using a serger looper threader to make threading the foot easier. If you're using a slotted foot, you will not need the threader.

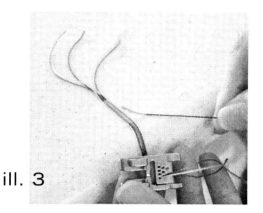

ill. 3

4. Attach the foot to the machine with the knot at the back of the foot. Insert a size 12/80 Universal or Machine Embroidery needle. Thread the machine with rayon embroidery thread. Insert a bobbin.

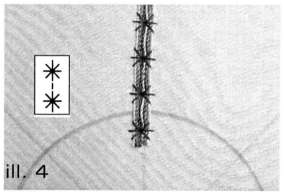

ill. 4

5. Select a stitch similar to the one we've pictured. Set the upper tension slightly lower than normal to ensure the bobbin thread does not pull to the top of your fabric. Beginning at the raw outer edge of the square, center the foot over one of your drawn lines and begin stitching your first row. Sew to approximately 1/2" inside the circle (ill. 4). Cut the cords and retie the ends (ill. 5 & 6). Repeat on all the drawn lines except the circle.

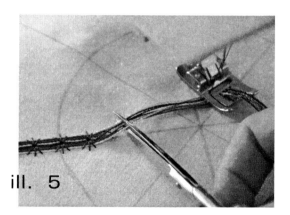

ill. 5

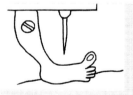 Having the presser foot in the down position while you cut will help prevent the cords from coming unthreaded from the foot.

6. Remove the multi-hole cording foot from the machine and reattach your standard sewing foot. Select the straight stitch and shorten the stitch length

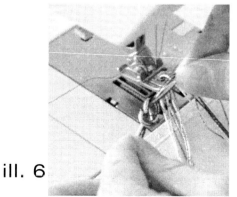

ill. 6

to 1.0. Set the upper tension back to normal for straight stitch sewing. Stitch across the ends of the cords to keep them from pulling out.

7. Remove the standard sewing foot and attach the open toe applique' foot. Select a stem-stitch, triple straight stitch or other similar stitch program. Thread the machine with rayon embroidery thread in the color of your choice. Position the fabric so that the inside of the right toe of the foot is riding along the edge of the outside cord. Sew one row (ill.7).

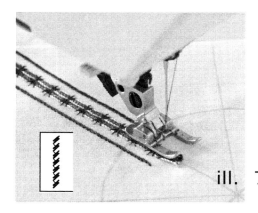

ill. 7

8. Sew a second row of the stem stitch on the opposite side of the cording.

 If your machine has mirror image capabil-ity, you may want to mirror image the sec-ond side or try pivoting your fab-ric and stitch from the opposite end to achieve a similar effect.

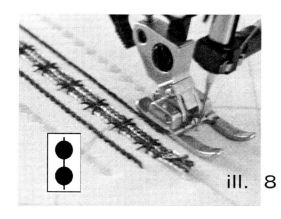

ill. 8

9. Change to another color of rayon embroidery thread. Select a round satin-stitch ball design or another similar stitch. Adjust the size to your liking. Using the outside edge of the foot as a guide, sew one row next to each of the previous rows (ill. 8).

10. Change to another color of rayon embroidery thread. Select a satin-stitch scallop. Adjust the size to your liking. Position the foot so that the left row of satin-stitch balls is along the inside edge of the right toe of the foot (ill. 9). Sew one row. Pivot the

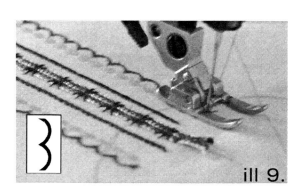

ill 9.

fabric and sew a row on the opposite side.

11. Use the template to trace the circle onto the paper side of fusible web. Press to the back of your fabric and cut out on the drawn line. Remove the paper backing and position the fabric in the center of the quilt block. Press in place.

12. Thread the machine with rayon embroidery thread to match the center circle fabric.

13. Set your machine for a 3.0mm wide satin stitch. We recommend a "z"-shaped zigzag if you have one available. This stitch formation tends to produce a more filled-in, uniform satin stitch and is especially good for applique' work. Stitch around the circle, pivoting slightly as needed to create a smooth circle. Be sure to tie off at the end of your stitching (ill. 10).

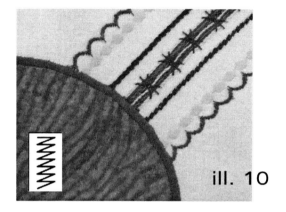

ill. 10

14. Trim block to 7 1/2" square and set aside.

GARDEN WALL

Supplies You'll Need

- Fagotting/Bridging Guide or Small Coffee Stir Straw
- Fringe Sewing Foot
- Couching/Braiding Foot
- Open Toe Applique' Foot
- 10" x 10" stabilized background fabric
- Size 80/12 Universal or Embroidery Needle
- Size 100 Topstitch needle
- Yellow 12-Weight cotton thread
- Monofilament thread
- Rayon embroidery thread
- 1" wide x 10" blue and yellow grosgrain ribbons
- 20" narrow rick rack or decorative cord
- Tear-away stabilizer
- Cellophane tape
- Small sharp scissors
- Tweezers
- Bobbin

---

1. Attach faggoting guide or tape 2 - 1" pieces of a small coffee stir straw centered directly in front of presser foot (ill. 1). See page 19 for stir straw details.

2. Attach the open toe applique' foot, insert a size 100 Topstitch needle and thread the machine with yellow 12-Weight thread on top and in the bobbin. Depending on your machine, you may have to hand-wind the 12-Weight thread onto a bobbin. Most machines can wind this thread just fine through the winding mechanism.

3. Select a decorative elastic zig-zag stitch similar to the one

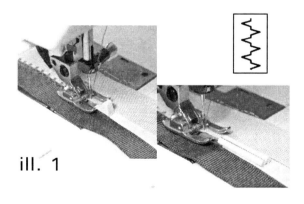

ill. 1

pictured - 6.0mm wide x 1.0mm length (ill 1.). Place the blue grosgrain ribbon on the left side of the guide and the yellow grosgrain ribbon on the right side of the guide. Stitch, making sure the outermost needle swing catches the edge of the ribbon. A "bridge" will be created as you sew the pieces together.

4. Align a second strip of yellow grosgrain ribbon on the opposite side of the blue ribbon. Repeat the bridging stitch to connect these together.

5. Insert the Universal or Embroidery needle. Thread the machine with monofilament thread. Insert a regular bobbin. Select a standard zigzag stitch - 2mm wide x 2mm long.

ill. 2

6. Center the ribbon band on the background fabric and pin in place.

7. Atach the couching/braiding foot. Feed narrow rick-rack or decorative ribbon through the guide/or guides on the foot (ill. 2). Attach the foot to the machine.

8. Center the foot on one yellow outer ribbon and zigzag in place through all thicknesses. Repeat for the second side (ill. 3).

9. Rethread the machine with rayon embroidery thread on top. Attach the fringe foot. Change the zigzag stitch width to 5-6 mm (depending on the width your machine can stitch) and the length to .25mm. Set the upper tension slightly looser than normal to ensure the bobbin thread doesn't pull to the top of your fabric.

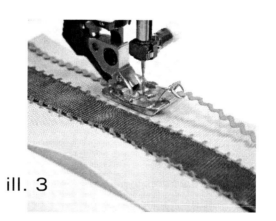

ill. 3

10. Place tear-away stabilizer under the fabric. Position the fabric

under the foot so that one side of the stitch is just catching the outside edge of the ribbon with most of the stitch falling on the background fabric (ill. 4).

ill. 4

11. Tie off at the beginning of the seam to keep the fringe from unraveling. Stitch along one side of the ribbon band and tie off at the end of the stitching. Repeat on the other side of the ribbon band.

12. Tape the fringe down to hold it out of the way for the next step - positioning the tape approximately 1/8" off the ribbon. (ill. 5).

13. Remove the fringe foot and attach your standard decorative stitch foot. Set your machine for a 3mm wide satin stitch.

ill. 5

14. Align the center of the foot with the edge of fringe that is on the ribbon. Satin-stitch over the fringe edge to secure. Repeat along the other row of fringe. (ill. 5).

15. From the back side of your project, use small sharp scissors to cut the bobbin thread and carefully pull the fringe to the top. Tweezers work well for this (ill. 6).

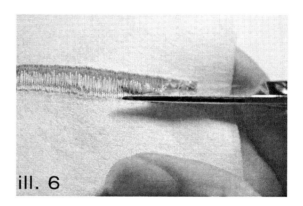

ill. 6

16. Trim block to 7 1/2" square and set aside.

TUMBLING BUBBLES

Supplies You'll Need

- Circular Embroidery Guide or Thumbtack
- Open Toe Appliqué Foot
- 10" x 10" background fabric
- Size 80/12 Universal or Embroidery needle
- Rayon embroidery thread - red, blue, yellow, green
- Tear-away or wash away stabilizer
- Fabric marker
- Bobbin

1. Insert the Universal or Embroidery needle. Attach the circle guide or thumbtack to create a 2" circle (1" from the needle). See page 15 for thumbtack details. Attach the open toe applique' Foot.

2. With a fabric marker, draw a line 2" in from the edge of the fabric. Draw a second line that intersects with the first 2" in from the adjacent edge. Position the guide or tack at the intersection point of the 2 lines (ill. 1).

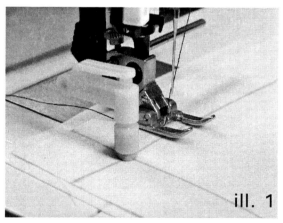

ill. 1

3. Thread the machine with yellow rayon embroidery thread (we've used dark thread for photo purposes only). Select one of your favorite decorative stitches. Place tear-away or wash-away stabilizer under the fabric. Sew a ¼ circle of the decorative stitch (ill. 2).

3. Reset the circle guide or thumbtack for a 3" circle

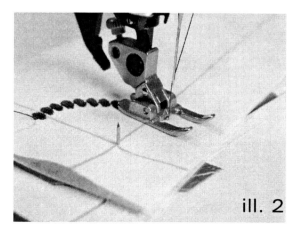

ill. 2

(1½" from the needle) and select another decorative stitch. Change to red rayon thread.

4. Position the tip of the circular guide or thumbtack on the same corner of the quilt block and sew a ¼ circle of the decorative stitch next to the first row.

5. Reset the circle guide for a 3½" circle (1¾" from the needle) and select another decorative stitch. Change to green rayon embroidery thread.

6. Position the tip of the circular guide or thumbtack on the same corner of the quilt block and sew a ¼ circle of the decorative stitch next to the second row.

7. Reset the circle guide or thumbtack for a 4" circle (2" from the needle) and select another decorative stitch. Change to blue rayon embroidery thread.

8. Position the tip of the circular guide or thumbtack on the same corner of the quilt block and sew a ¼ circle of the decorative stitch next to the third row to complete the corner motif.

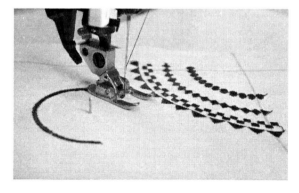

ill.   3

9. Reset the circle guide or thumbtack for a 2" circle (1" from the needle) and select a zigzag stitch. Set the stitch width at 2 and the stitch length for a satin stitch. Test on a scrap of fabric to achieve the look you desire.

10. With blue thread still on the machine, sew 2 or 3 circles randomly on the quilt block (ill. 3).

11. Repeat with red, green and yellow thread to have overlapping "tumbling" circles.

12. Trim block to 7 1/2" square. Set aside.

HOW DOES YOUR GARDEN GROW?

Supplies You'll Need

- Open Toe Appliqué Foot
- Rolled Hem Foot
- Multi-Hole Cording Foot
- Narrow Edge/Edge Joining Foot
- Fringe Sewing Foot
- 10" x 10" stabilized background fabric
- 4 - 3" x 3" red fabric
- 2 - 2" x 8" green fabric
- 3 - 1 1/2" x 12" yellow fabric
- Size 80/12 Universal or Embroidery needle
- Rayon embroidery thread (yellow, red, green)
- Regular sewing thread
- 1/4" finished width green bias
- #34 gauge wire
- Wire cutters
- Gimp thread
- 5 - 1/2" buttons
- Fusible web
- Fabric marker
- Water-soluble Stabilizer
- Bobbin
- Flower stems pattern (at end of book)

1. Fuse two pieces of the red fabric wrong sides together with fusible web. With a fabric marker, trace the flower pattern onto one side of the fabric (at end of book).

2. Attach the open toe foot and insert the Universal or Embroidery needle. Thread the machine with red rayon thread.

3. Select a zigzag stitch. Set the stitch width to 1.5 and the stitch length to 1.5.

4. Position #34 gauge wire on the line (ill. 1). Zigzag over the wire along the drawn line. Use

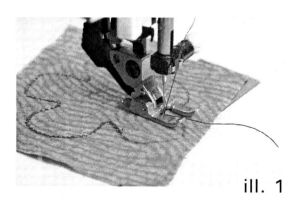

ill. 1

wire cutters to cut off the excess wire.

5. Cut out flower close to stitching. Place water-soluble stabilizer under flower. Set machine for a 3mm wide satin stitch. Satin stitch over previous stitching, making sure right swing of the needle falls off the fabric and into stabilizer. Cut off excess stabilizer and set aside (ill. 2). Repeat to create second flower.

6. Fuse the two pieces of green fabric wrong sides together with fusible web. With a fabric marker, trace 5 leaves onto the right side of the green fabric using the provided pattern.

7. Change the upper thread to green. Position #34 gauge wire on the line of one leaf. Zigzag (1.5mm x 1.5mm) over the wire along the drawn line. Use wire cutters to cut off the excess wire. Cut out leaf and satin stitch as for flower. Repeat for the remaining leaves. Set aside.

8. Attach the rolled hem foot to the machine. Thread the machine with yellow rayon thread on the top.

9. Roll hem one long side of each of the 1 1/2" x 12" pieces of yellow fabric (ill. 3).

10. Rethread machine with regular sewing thread. Attach the multi-hole cording foot to the machine. Thread 2 - 18" lengths of gimp cord into the holes that fall left and right of center.

11. Select a two step zigzag stitch. Change the stitch length to 3.0 and set the width wide enough to stitch over the 2 cords without catching the cord. Align the

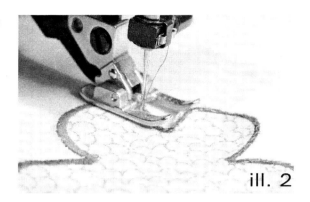

ill. 2

ill. 3

right edge of the foot with the raw edge of the fabric. Couch the gimp cord to the long unfinished edge of the fabric, making sure not to catch the cord in the stitching (ill. 4).

12. Pull the cords from one end to gather the fabric as tightly as possible. Tie-off the cords on both ends to secure. With right sides together, sew across the short end of the fabric, making sure to tie-off at beginning and end of seam. Backstitch across the cords a number of times to ensure the cords won't pull out. Zigzag (1.5 x 1.5mm) close to straight stitching to finish raw edge. Trim excess fabric. Repeat for second and third flower (ill. 5).

13. Using the pattern at the end of the book, draw 5 stems on the background fabric. Position the leaves randomly along the lines and pin in place.

14. Thread machine with green rayon thread. Lay green bias strips over the lines and pin in place. Make sure that the bottom edges of the leaves are under the bias strip.

15. Attach the narrow edge foot to the machine. Select straight stitch and stitch along both sides of each bias strip, catching the bottom edge of the leaves under the stitching. Make sure you remove the pins as you come to them. Sewing over pins can damage your needle. Change the needle position if necessary (ill. 6).

16. Position the wire edge flower at the top of the center stem. Select the button attaching stitch or zigzag stitch. Drop the feed dogs. Set the the width of the stitch wide enough so the needle swing falls in the holes of

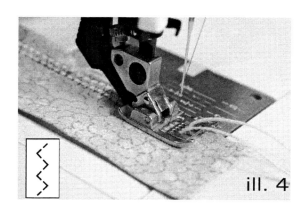

ill. 4

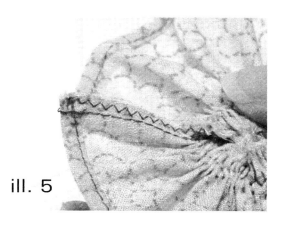

ill. 5

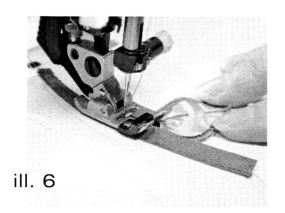

ill. 6

the button. Center a button over the flower and stitch in place (ill. 7). Repeat for the 2nd wire-edged flower.

ill. 7

17. Position one gathered flower over one of the remaining stems and center the button over the flower. Stitch in place. Repeat for the remaining flowers.

18. With a fabric marker, draw a line across the bottom of the fabric ¾" from the bottom edge.

19. Attach the fringe foot to the machine. Thread the machine with green rayon thread on top.

20. Select the zigzag stitch. Change the width to 6.0 or as wide as your fringe foot will allow. Change the length to sew a tight satin stitch.

21. Center the foot over the line and zigzag across the bottom of the fabric. Be sure to tie off at the beginning and end of the stitching.

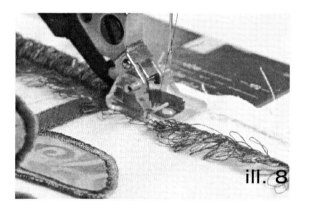

ill. 8

22. Attach the standard sewing foot. Change the stitch width to 2.0. Stitch along the bottom edge of the fringe to secure.

23. Attach the fringe foot to the machine and position the fabric with the edge of the foot touching the bottom of the previously fringed row (ill. 8). Change the stitch width to 6.0. Sew a second row of fringe, overlapping the foot slightly so the left swing of the needle just touches the bottom of the first row. Secure with the zigzag stitch as above.

24. Turn the fabric over and cut the bobbin thread across each row of fringe. Pull the fringe to the top to create "grass" (ill. 9).

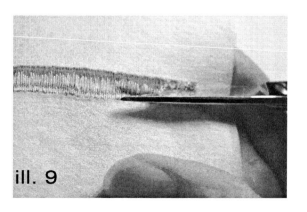

ill. 9

25. Trim block to 7 1/2" square and set aside.

LAZY DAISIES

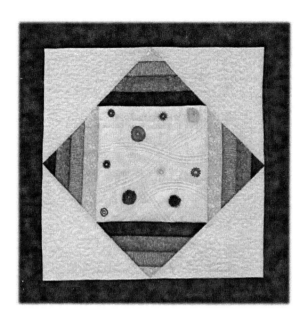

Supplies you'll need

- Pintuck Foot
- Eyelet Plate
- 12" x 12" lightly stabilized background fabric
- Size 80/12 Universal or Embroidery needle
- Size 2.0/80 Twin needle
- 2 spools standard sewing thread
- Rayon embroidery thread
- Bobbin
- Gimp cord
- Fabric marker
- 5" spring embroidery hoop
- Small sharp scissors
- Tweezers (optional)

If an eyelet plate is not available for your particular machine/model, substitute single stitched motifs of your choice.

Pintucks

1. If your machine has a needle plate with a hole at the center front, remove the needleplate from the machine and insert the gimp cord through the hole from the bottom to the top. Reattach the plate to your machine (ill. 1).

-OR-

If your needleplate does not have a hole for cord to pass through, you can put a coffee stir straw to work for you...see page 18 for details on stir straw corded pintucks. (ill. 2).

2. Insert a size 2.0/80 twin needle. Using your second spoolpin or an accessory spool pin, thread the machine with 2 spools of 100% cotton construction

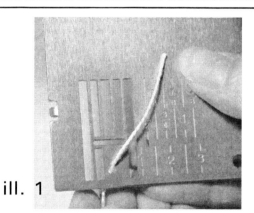

ill. 1

ill. 2

thread. Thread the machine, placing one thread to the right and one thread to the left of the tension disk. Thread the needle eyes. Insert a bobbin.

3. Attach your pintuck foot. Test sew a pintuck on a scrap of your fabric. Make sure that the gimp cord is feeding straight out the back of the machine and is centered between the 2 needles as you begin to sew. This will ensure that the cord is encased at the beginning of the tuck.

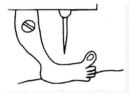 You should not need to adjust your tension. However, if your pintucks are not forming quite as crisply as you'd like, tighten the upper tension just slightly tighter than normal. Do not over-tighten as this will typically cause puckered pintucks.

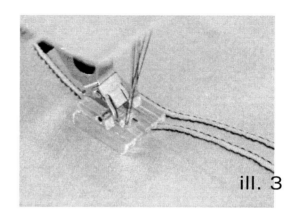

ill. 3

4. On your 12" x 12" fabric, "meander" with gentle curves as you sew the pintucks. After you have completed one tuck, position that sewn tuck in one of the outer grooves to sew the next pintuck. This will ensure that your pintucks are evenly spaced. Sew several sets of 3 pintucks (ill. 3).

Eyelets

1. Lower the feed dogs.

2. Remove the sewing foot and attach the eyelet plate. If an eyelet plate is not available for your particular model, select your favorite decorative stitches and sew single repeats of them where the eyelets would be

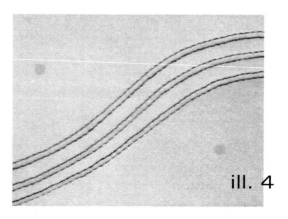

ill. 4

placed.

3. Remove the twin needle and insert the Universal or Embroidery needle. Thread the machine with rayon embroidery thread on top. Set the tension slightly looser than normal to make sure the bobbin thread doesn't pull to the top surface of your fabric.

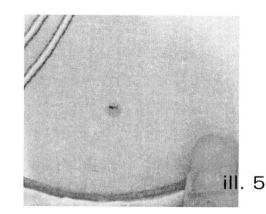

ill. 5

4. With a fabric marker, place small dots on the fabric where you would like eyelets. See the sample for suggested placement (ill.4).

5. Hoop your fabric, making sure it is taut. This is very important for successful eyelets.

6. With small sharp scissors, cut one or two threads at each dot - just enough to create a tiny little hole to allow you to push the fabric over the pin of the eyelet plate. The fabric must fit tightly around the pin (ill. 5).

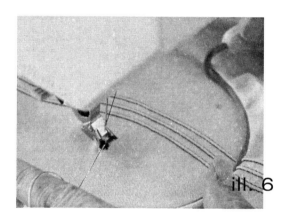

ill. 6

7. Set the presser foot lifter into the darning or free-motion position for your machine.

8. To create the "fuzzy" eyelets, select a standard zigzag stitch and set the width to the widest setting for your machine. Stitch length does not matter as you will be controlling this. Pull up the bobbin thread and hold both threads for the first few stitches then trim these threads (ill. 6).

9. Sew by pivoting the hoop in a slow and even motion around the center hole (ill. 7). Sew at a medium speed. When you need to reposition your hands, make sure you stop sewing - this will help ensure that your eyelets are consistent and even.

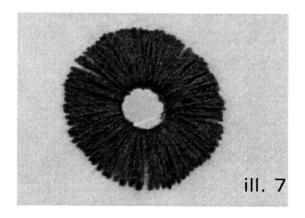

ill. 7

10. Select a right/left needle position zigzag and set at 2 - 2.5mm wide. (ill. 8) Set your machine so the needle begins stitching in the far left. Stitch slowly and evenly around the eyelet so that all previously sewn stitches are secured. This adds a narrow satin stitch that covers the inner edge of the eyelet, securing the fringe. To tie off, select the straight stich and sew a few stitches in place. If necessary, move the needle position to do this.

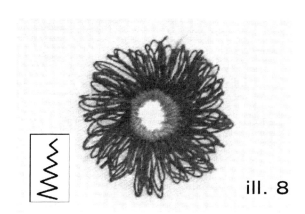

ill. 8

11. Remove the hoop from the machine. Do not remove the fabric from the hoop.

12. From the wrong side, cut the bobbin thread using small sharp scissors. Pull the rayon thread to the top. Tweezers work well for this. Repeat for the desired number of "fuzzy" eyelets.

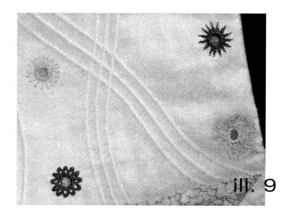

ill. 9

13. To create decorative eyelets, select a patterned stitch program. Several different looks can be created by changing the stitch length and by moving the hoop at different speeds. Scallops stitch patterns, the blind hem stitch and the stretch blind hem stitch are good choices. Mirror images create a different design (ill. 9).

Use stitches similar to those pictured (ill. 10).

Experiment, experiment, experiment!

14. Scatter several decorative eyelets on your quilt block.

15. Trim block to 7 1/2" square and set aside.

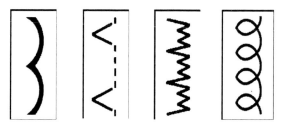

ill. 10

GARDEN HEDGE

Supplies You'll Need

- Narrow Edge/Edge Joining Foot
- Circular Embroidery Guide or Thumbtack/Tape
- Couching/Braiding Foot
- Open Toe Appliqué Foot
- Gathering/Shirring Foot
- Bias Binder (or rolled hem foot if a bias binder is not available for your machine)
- 10" x 10" background fabric
- 2 - 3" x 15" green fabric for ruffle
- Size 80/12 Universal or Embroidery needle
- Rayon embroidery thread - red, blue, yellow, green
- Monofilament thread
- Tear-away stabilizer
- 10" x 1/8" gold decorative cord
- 10" x 1/8" red decorative cord
- 20" - 1/4" wide blue satin ribbon
- 20" - 1/4" wide strip of blue bias cut fabric
- Bobbin
- Fabric marker

1. With a fabric marker, draw a line down the center of the background fabric from top to bottom. Draw a line 2 1/2" on either side of the center line. Place a mark 3" down from one edge on each outer line (ill. 1).

2. Insert Universal or Embroidery needle. Attach the circle guide or thumbtack to create a 2" circle. See page 15 for thumbtack details.

3. Attach the open toe applique' foot. Position the tip of the circle guide or thumbtack at one of the marked points

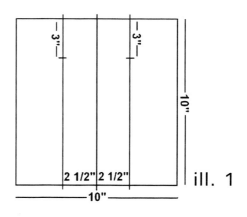

ill. 1

on the outer lines. Thread the machine with red rayon thread. Select one of your favorite decorative stitches (we used a small satin stitched ball). Place tear-away stabilizer under the fabric. Position the needle on the line and sew a half circle back to the line (ill. 2).

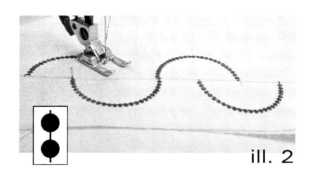

ill. 2

4. Reposition the tip of the circle guide (or thumbtack) at the end of the half circle that you just sewed and sew a half circle on the opposite side of the line. Reposition guide (or thumbtack) so the point of the needle is positioned at the end of the previous half circle and the guide (or tack) is on the line. Stitch the third half circle. Reposition the guide (or tack) at the end of the third half circle and stitch the final half circle. Change to yellow rayon thread and repeat on 2nd outer line (ill. 2).

5. Attach the narrow edge/edge joining foot. Thread the machine with blue decorative rayon thread. Lay the blue satin ribbon over the right drawn line at the center of one row of half-circles. Stitch down both sides with a straight stitch. Change the needle position, if necessary, to stitch as close to the edge as possible. Repeat for the other group of circles (ill. 3). Remove all excess stabilizer.

ill. 3

6. Rethread machine with green rayon thread. Attach the bias binder to your machine. Adjust the bias binder or needle position so the stitching falls close to the inner edge of the binding fabric.

7. Select a straight stitch with a length of 2.5. A zigzag or blanket stitch may also be used for a

more decorative effect...but only if your foot has a wide needle opening.

8. To feed the bias strip into the foot, cut a right angle at the leading end and feed into the scroll of the foot. You may find this easier to do before attaching the foot to the machine. A straight pin is very useful for helping to pull the end of the fabric through the binder (ill. 4). To get the bias started, stitch a length approximately 1 1/2". Leave end of bias under presser foot.

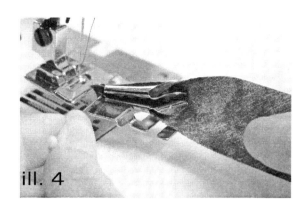

ill. 4

9. Place the 2 green fabrics, wrong sides together, into the slot of the bias binder so that they are against the inner curve of the guide & butted against the binding fabric. Use your left hand to guide the fabric and your right hand to guide the binding. The fabric will be at a fairly sharp angle as it enters the foot. Sew the bias binding to both sides of the double-layer green fabric strip (ill. 5).

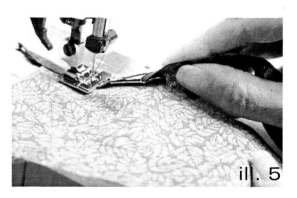

ill. 5

10. Attach the gathering/shirring foot. Select a long straight stitch and tighten the upper tension almost as tight as it will go. Test the gathering on a double-layer scrap of fabric. Your 15" strip of fabric should gather down to approximately 9-10" (ill. 6). And...don't torture yourself too much if your gathers aren't this tight...simply cut off the excess fabric after you've attached it to the base fabric!

11. With a fabric marker, draw a line down the center of your green bound strip. Center the strip under the needle. Sew down the middle of the green strip, allowing it to gather as much as

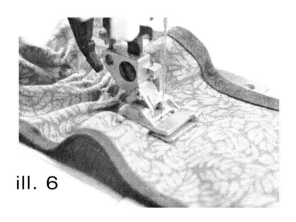

ill. 6

possible.

12. Center the gathered fabric strip on the center line on the background fabric. Pin in place. Adjust the gathers as needed.

13. Attach the couching/braiding foot to the machine. Thread the machine with monofilament thread.

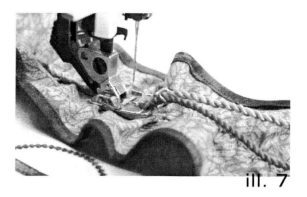

ill. 7

15. Feed the red and gold decorative cords together through the guide on the foot. Select the zigzag stitch and set the width to a setting wide enough to clear the braid. Set the stitch length to 3.0mm or longer. Position the background block with the green fabric strip under the foot and sew down the middle of the green strip, couching the braid in place (ill. 7). For a different effect, try twisting the braids as they go through the front of the foot (ill. 8).

16. Trim the finished block to 7 1/2" square. Set the block aside.

ill. 8

STEPPING STONES

Supplies You'll Need

- Circular Embroidery Guide or Thumbtack
- Open Toe Appliqué Foot
- 10" x 10" background fabric
- Size 80/12 Universal or Embroidery needle
- Rayon embroidery thread - red, blue, yellow, green
- Bobbin
- Fabric Marker
- Bobbin

1. Attach the circle guide or thumbtack to your sewing machine to create a 2" circle. See page 15 for thumbtack details. Attach the foot.

2. With a fabric marker, draw a vertical line through the center of the 10" x 10" fabric. Draw lines on either side of this 3 1/2" away. Draw a horizontal line through the center of the block. Draw lines on either side of this line 3 1/2" away. This will create an intersecting line at the center and four corners of the block (ill. 1).

3. Thread the machine with yellow rayon embroidery thread.

4. Position the circular guide or thumbtack on the intersecting point at the center of the block. Select one of your favorite decorative stitches and sew a complete circle of the stitches (ill. 2).

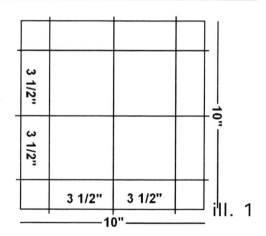

ill. 1

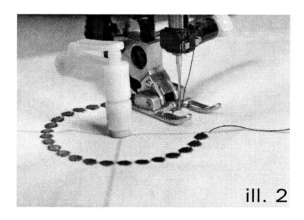

ill. 2

5. Position the tip of the circular guide or thumbtack on one corner intersecting point of the quilt block and sew a ¼ circle of the same decorative stitch. Repeat on the remaining 3 corners (ill. 3).

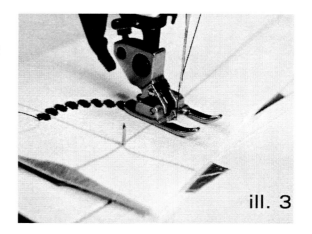

ill. 3

6. Reset the circle guide for a 3" circle (1 1/2" from the needle) and select another decorative stitch. Change to red rayon embroidery thread. Sew a circle of stitches around the first circle at the center of the block.

7. Position the tip of the circular guide on one corner of the quilt block and sew a ¼ circle of the same decorative stitch. Repeat on the remaining 3 corners.

8. Reset the circle guide for a 3½" circle (1 3/4" from the needle) and select another decorative stitch. Change to green rayon embroidery thread. Sew a circle of stitches around the second circle in the center of the block.

9. Position the tip of the circular guide on one corner of the quilt block and sew a ¼ circle of the same decorative stitch. Repeat on the remaining 3 corners.

10. Reset the circle guide for a 4" circle (2" from the needle) and select another decorative stitch. Change to blue rayon embroidery thread. Sew a circle of stitches around the third circle in the center of the block.

11. Position the tip of the circular guide on one corner of the quilt block and sew a ¼ circle of the same decorative stitch. Repeat on the remaining 3 corners.

12. Trim block to 7 1/2" square and set aside.

GARDEN PATCH

Supplies You'll Need

- Pintuck Foot
- Pintuck Foot With Guide (if available)
- Open Toe Appliqué Foot
- Cording Blade or Round Toothpick
- 12" x 12" back ground fabric
- Size 2.0/80 twin needle
- Size 80/12 Universal or Embroidery needle
- 2 spools of standard sewing thread to match fabric
- Rayon embroidery thread
- Bobbin
- Tear-away stabilizer

1. Insert the size 2.0/80 twin needle. Thread the machine with 2 spools of standard sewing thread, placing one thread to the right and one thread to the left of the tension disk. Thread the needles.

2. Snap the cording blade into place or tape a round toothpick centered in front of the presser foot. See page 16 for thumbtack details. The cording blade/toothpick will help create a deeper and more defined tuck (ill. 1).

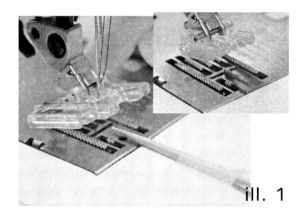

ill. 1

3. Attach the pintuck foot. Select the straight stitch and set the tension approx. 1 number higher than normal. For instance, if your standard tension is 4, set your upper tension at 5. A slightly tighter tension will create a more prominent tuck.

4. Press a line along the center of

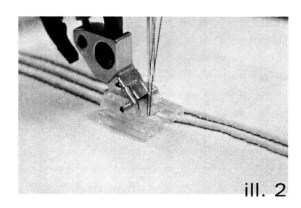

ill. 2

the background fabric from top to bottom as a guide for the first tuck. Position the pressed line under the center guide of the foot between the two needles and sew one tuck.

5. Reposition the sewn tuck into the far right guide of the foot and sew a second tuck. Reposition the first sewn tuck into the far left guide and sew a third pin-tuck (ill. 2).

6. Remove the pintuck foot and attach the pintuck foot with guide (if available).

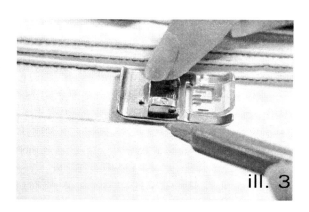

ill. 3

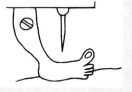 If a pintuck foot with guide is not available for your machine, simply leave a space between pintucks that is wide enough for a decorative stitch to be sewn. The width of your presser foot is a good width to use (ill. 3), Sew decorative stitches in the wide space between the groups of pintucks.

7. Position the right sewn pintuck into the guide on the extension and sew one tuck (ill. 4). Pivot the fabric and sew another pin-tuck on the opposite side. This will create channels for decora-tive stitching.

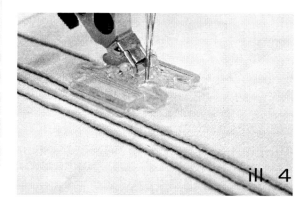

ill. 4

8. Attach the pintuck foot, align the single pintuck in the outer left groove and sew two more pintucks to create a second 3-pintuck section. Repeat to create a third 3-pintuck group on the opposite side of the original 3 tucks (ill. 5).

9. Insert the needle. Attach the pin-tuck foot with guide (or decora-tive stitch foot or open toe foot) to the machine.

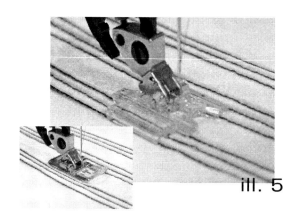

ill. 5

10. Thread the machine with rayon embroidery thread. Select a stitch program of your choice. Place tear-away stabilizer under the fabric and position two pintucks in the grooves to the right and left of center so the wide space is centered under the foot. This allows the pintucks to track so that the decorative stitching is perfectly centered (ill. 6 & 7). Sew decorative stitches in each channel and along the outer edge of the tucks.

11. To sew the scalloped border, position the outer pintuck in the extension on the foot or align the edge of the decorative stitch foot or open toe foot next to the outer pintuck.

12. Trim block to 7 1/2" square and set aside.

ill. 6

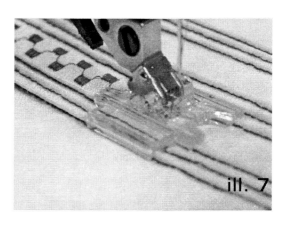

ill. 7

ASSEMBLY

Supplies You'll Need

- Narrow Edge/Edge Joining Foot
- 1/4" Quilting Foot
- Free Motion Quilting Foot or Darning Foot
- 5 each - 1 3/8" x fabric width strips of blue, green, red and yellow fabrics
- 9 - 13" squares of background fabric
- 9 - 2½" x 45" wide strips blue fabric
- 5 - 2" x 45" wide crossgrain strips of green fabric (substitute bias following the instructions on page 20 Continuous Bias)
- 1 - 4" x 45" backing fabric for rod pocket
- 56" x 56" Backing fabric
- Size 80/12 Universal needle
- Quilting Needle
- Standard sewing thread for needle and bobbin

1. Remove all stabilizer. Attach the ¼" quilting foot. Using the long 1 3/8" wide strips, sew a blue strip to a green strip with a ¼" seam. Add a red strip to the blue strip. Add a yellow strip to the red strip. Make a total of 5 strip-pieced sets in the same color order (ill. 1).

2. Cut 45° triangles across one strip set by placing the 45° angle marking of your ruler on the lower edge of one of the strips and cutting with a rotary cutter. Reposition the ruler to cut the opposite side of the triangle (ill. 2). Continue alternating up and down with all 5 strips to create 18 triangles with the blue on the top and 18 triangles with the blue on the bottom.

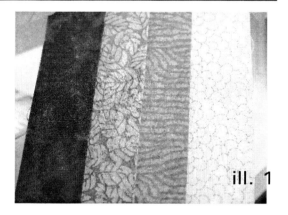

ill. 1

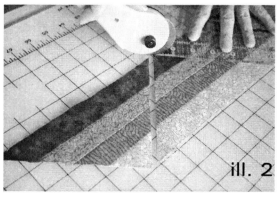

ill. 2

3. Sew the triangles with the blue on the bottom to the top and bottom of each quilt block. Sew the triangles with the blue on the top to the right and left side of each quilt block (ill 3).

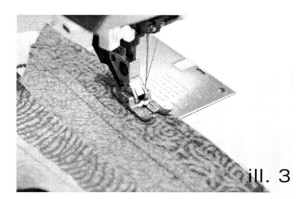

ill. 3

4. On the 13" squares of background fabric, draw diagonal lines from corner to corner that intersect at the center of the square. Rotary cut on these lines to create four triangles from each square. You'll have a total of 36 triangles. Sew these triangles to the four sides of each quilt block (ill. 4). Trim blocks to 14" square.

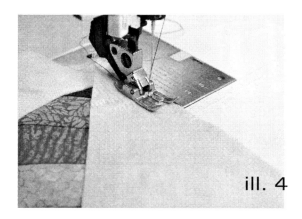

ill. 4

5. Cut 9 sashing strips of blue fabric 2½" x width of fabric. From this, cut 6 - 14" long strips. Set the rest aside.

6. To create the first row of the quilt, sew Garden Path to Sunburst together with a sashing strip in between. Sew Sunburst to Garden Wall with the sashing in between (ill. 5).

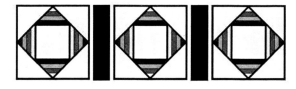

ill. 5

7. Create row 2 of the quilt by sewing Tumbling Bubbles, How Does Your Garden Grow and Lazy Daisies with sashing in between.

8. Create row 3 of the quilt by sewing Garden Hedge, Stepping Stones and Garden Patch with sashing in between.

9. The remaining blue strips will need to be pieced. Trim off the selvedges and place the ends of 2 strips right sides together at right angles. Draw a 45° line for stitching. Sew the strips together on this line. Trim off excess fabric leaving a ¼" seam. Press seam to one side (ill. 6).

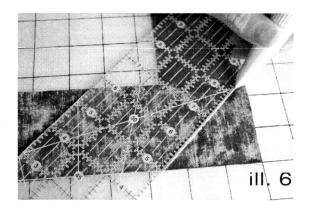

ill. 6

10. Measure across the width of the first row of blocks at the center. This measurement is the length your sashing strips need to be cut. Cut 4 sashing strips to this length. To attach the sashing to the top of the first row of blocks, find the center of the top edge of the row and pin the center of one sashing strip at this point. Pin the ends of the strips to the ends of the block row. Sew in place, gently easing if needed. Attaching the sashing in this way helps to assure that your quilt will be truly square and prevent a "rippling" affect on the edges of your quilt.

11. Following the above steps, sew row one to row 2 with one strip and row 2 to row 3 with another. Sew a strip to the bottom of row 3 (ill. 7).

12. Sew a sashing strip to each side again using the measure from center method, and cutting the 2 side sashing strips the same length (ill. 8).

13. Cut a piece of batting and a piece of backing fabric 2" larger all the way around than the quilt top. You may need to piece fabric to make a backing wide enough for your quilt. If you must piece your backing, use a full fabric width in the center and add narrower pieces to the sides. This will eliminate a center seam down the back of your quilt.

14. To make a rod pocket on the back of the quilt, press under a double fold ½" hem on the short ends of a 4" x 45" piece of fabric. Press and stitch the hem.

15. Press the fabric in half length-

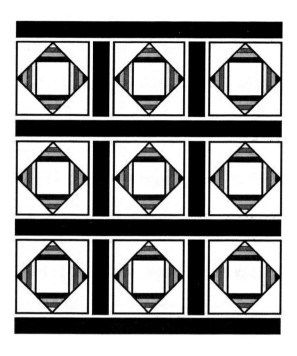

ill. 7

ill. 8

wise. Center the rod pocket on the wrong side of the quilt backing, aligning the raw edges of the pocket piece with the raw edge of the quilt backing. Open out the folded fabric and stitch along the fold line to secure the pocket piece to the back of the quilt (ill. 9). Press the pocket fabric back up into place, realigning the raw edges. Baste a 1/4" seam across the top to secure all 3 layers together.

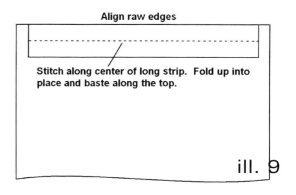

Align raw edges

Stitch along center of long strip. Fold up into place and baste along the top.

ill. 9

16. Lay the backing fabric wrong side up on a table large enough for the entire quilt or on an empty area of your floor. Use masking tape to secure the backing fabric to the table or floor. Lay the batting and the quilt front on top of the backing fabric. You should have a fairly even amount of batting and backing fabric extending beyond your quilt top.

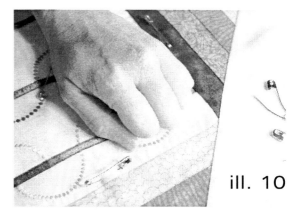

ill. 10

17. Starting in the center of your quilt, pin-baste the layers together leaving about a fist-width space between pins (ill. 10).

17. Attach the edge joining/narrow edge foot and "stitch in the ditch" around each of the blocks and on all seam lines (ill. 11). See page 22 for details.

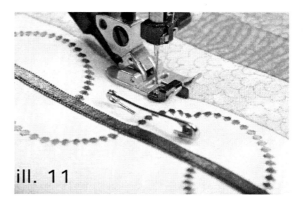

ill. 11

18. Attach the free-motion foot and stipple quilt the triangles of background fabric (ill. 12). If you've never stippled before, see Stipple Quilting on page 21 for setup steps.

19. Square up the quilt top and trim excess batting and backing to same size as quilt top using a rotary cutter, mat & ruler.

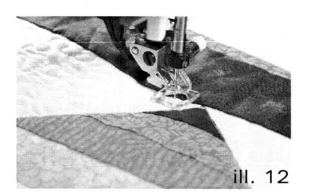

ill. 12

20. <u>If you prefer to create bias for the binding:</u>

See Circle Secrets & Other Slick Tips, page 20 Making Continuous Bias. You will need approximately 220" of binding.

<u>To use crossgrain cut binding strips:</u>

Cut 2" wide strips across the width of your fabric. You will need approximately 200" of binding. Cut ends of strips on a 45° angle (bias strips will already have angled ends). Sew strips together to form one long binding strip.

Whichever binding method you choose, fold the binding strip in half lengthwise, matching raw edges. Press.

21. Attach the 1/4" Quilting Foot.

22 Beginning at the center of the bottom edge of your quilt, match raw edges of binding and quilt, folding beginning end of binding at a 45° angle (ill. 13). Stitch using a ¼" seam. Continue sewing to corner. When you are ¼" from corner of quilt, stop with your needle in the fabric. Raise the presser foot and pivot your fabric on a 45° angle towards the outer corner of the quilt, lower your presser foot and stitch to the outer corner of the quilt (ill. 13). This little angled seam will give you a nice fold line to aid in forming your mitered corner.

23. Remove quilt from machine and fold the binding strip up along the corner seam (ill. 14).

24. Fold the binding strip back on itself, even with the edges of your quilt and stitch using a ¼"

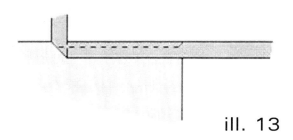

ill. 13

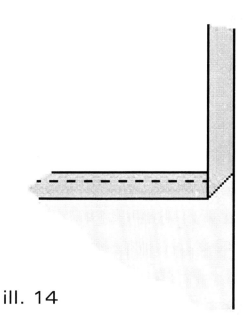

ill. 14

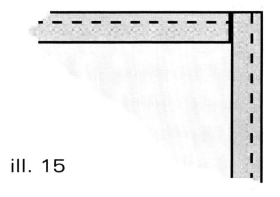

ill. 15

seam allowance (ill. 15). Sew
to the next corner and repeat.
Continue in this manner until
you reach the beginning of your
binding.

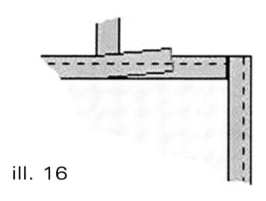

ill. 16

25. Cut the end of the binding strip
so it overlaps the beginning
approximately 3". Overlap end
of binding strip at a slight angle
over beginning point of binding
strip. Continue stitching across
to secure (ill. 16) Trim uneven
raw edges/tails of binding.

26. Turn binding strip to wrong side
of quilt, finger-pressing corners
to a nice sharp point. Lightly
press. Set machine for a very
tiny zigzag stitch (1.5mm x
1.5mm).

 Adjust the
width/length of
your zigzag as
desired. You
may also use
a blindhem or
blanket stitch in place of the zigzag.
The tiny zigzag stitch does tend to
be the strongest/most secure.

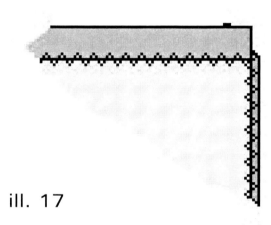

ill. 17

27. From wrong side of quilt, fold
back one long edge of binding strip so only a tiny (1/8" or
less) bit of the binding is showing. Zigzag so the left swing of
the needle is biting only slightly
into the backing/batting of your
quilt and the right swing of the
needle stitches in air on the right
side of the quilt binding (ill. 17).
Tie-off at beginning and end
of seam. Repeat for remaining
sides. Lightly press to flatten
binding (ill. 18).

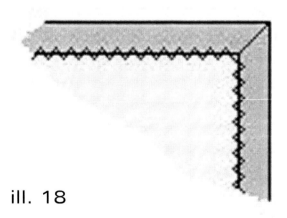

ill. 18

28. And, last but certainly not least,
add a quilt label to the back
of your quilt or sign your quilt
using a permanent fabric marker.

THROW PILLOW

Supplies You'll Need

The supplies listed are only the additional supplies to complete a throw pillow. You'll also need the supplies to complete the block of your choice (see individual chapters for these).

- Completed quilt block of your choice
- Piping/Cording/Knit Edge foot
- Standard sewing foot
- Narrow Edge/Edge Joining Foot
- 1/4" Quilting foot
- 23" Square Quilt Batting
- 2 - 20" x 23" Square Backing Fabric
- 2½" yards 5/32" cording
- Pillow form or fiberfill to make your own (instructions are included at the end of the section)
- 2 - 3" x 45" wide strips green fabric
- 4 - 3" x 3" squares red fabric for cornerstones
- 90" x 1½" wide green or red bias strip for piping

Any one of the blocks in this quilt would make a great pillow. To make into a pillow, follow the instructions in the Assembly section to complete the block to the point of adding the background fabric to the outside corners.

You may add sashing to the pillow in the same way as the quilt or you might like to add cornerstones for a different affect.

To add cornerstones to your pillow top:

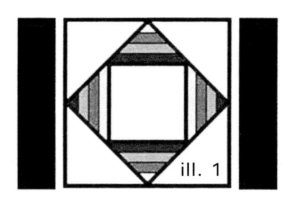

ill. 1

1. Cut two strips of green fabric 3" x the width of the fabric. Measure one side of the quilt block (it should be approximately 15½"). Cut 4 strips to this length from the long blue strips. Cut 4 - 3" x 3" squares from the red fabric.

2. Using the 1/4" quilting foot, sew two of the blue strips to the sides of the quilt block (ill. 1).

3. Sew the 3" squares to the ends of the remaining two blue strips. Sew these strips to the top and bottom of the quilt block (ill. 2).

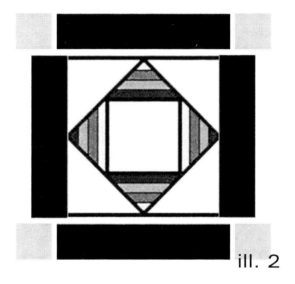

ill. 2

4. Lay the muslin wrong side up on the table and layer the batting and quilt block on top. Pin baste.

5. Stitch in the ditch and free-motion quilt as desired. See pages 21 & 22 for details.

6. Square up block, cutting through all three layers (top, batting & muslin.

7. To create piping for the pillow edge, cut green fabric into bias strips 1½" wide. See Circle Secrets and Other Slick Tips (beginning on page 15) for making continuous bias. You will need approximately 90" of bias.

8. Attach the piping foot to your machine. Wrap the bias strip around the 5/32 cord and stitch close to the cord (ill. 3). If you can change needle positions on your machine, this is a good time to use that feature, stitching very close to the piping.

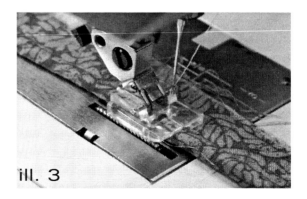

ill. 3

9. Trim the seam allowance on the piping to ¼". Starting at the bottom center of the quilt block, align the raw edge of the piping with the raw edge of the quilt block leaving a 3" tale on the piping (ill. 4).

ill. 4

10. Sew the piping to the quilt block. Moving your needle one position closer to the cord than you used to create the piping will keep that first row of stitching from showing on the front of your pillow. If you cannot change your needle position, sew one thread closer to the piping. Half an inch from the corner, change the stitch length to 0.5mm. Stop stitching 1/4" from the corner and clip the piping seam allowance up to the stitching line (ill. 5). Turn the corner, realign the raw edges and sew for ½" more before returning the stitch length to normal. Continue sewing to the next corner and repeat.

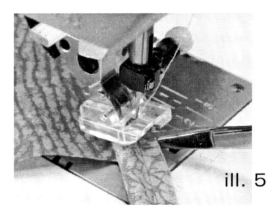

ill. 5

11. When you reach the beginning, gently push the fabric casing back from the piping cord and remove the cord where the piping will overlap. Do this on both ends of the piping (ill. 6). Overlap the ends and sew in place (ill. 7). If you are experienced at inserting piping, you may wish to create and insert the piping in one step.

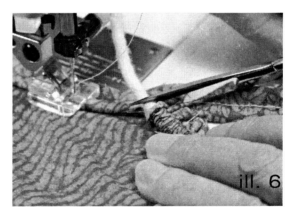

ill. 6

12. Cut two pieces of blue fabric 23" x 20". Clean finish one 20" edge of each fabric piece by pressing under a double fold ½" hem and stitching in place.

13. With right sides face up, overlap the finished edges by 6". Pin or baste along the overlapped edges to hold the 2 layers together. This will create the overlap opening for inserting the

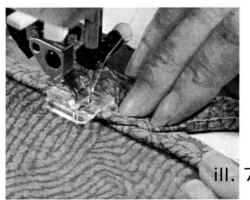

ill. 7

pillow form. Measure the pillow front and cut the back to that size.

14. Lay the back and front right sides together and stitch around the pillow as close to the piping as possible. Trim the excess fabric from the curves and turn right side out.

15. Insert purchased pillow form or make your own from muslin and fiberfill.

To make your own pillow form:

- Cut two pieces of quilt batting 1" larger all the way around than the finished size of your pillow.

- Sew the 2 pieces together, leaving an opening for turning. Stuff the pillow form with polyester fiberfill and stitch closed. Insert into the pillow.

WALLHANGING

The three blocks used for the wallhanging are Sunburst, How Does Your Garden Grow and Lazy Daisies. We created a sunburst block using only half the sun and a half-size version of the Lazy Daisies. The How Does Your Garden Grow block uses 3 flowers instead of 5.

The pattern for the half sun is located at the back of the book. For the stem placement use the pattern at the back of the book, eliminating stems 2 & 4.

STEMS PATTERN

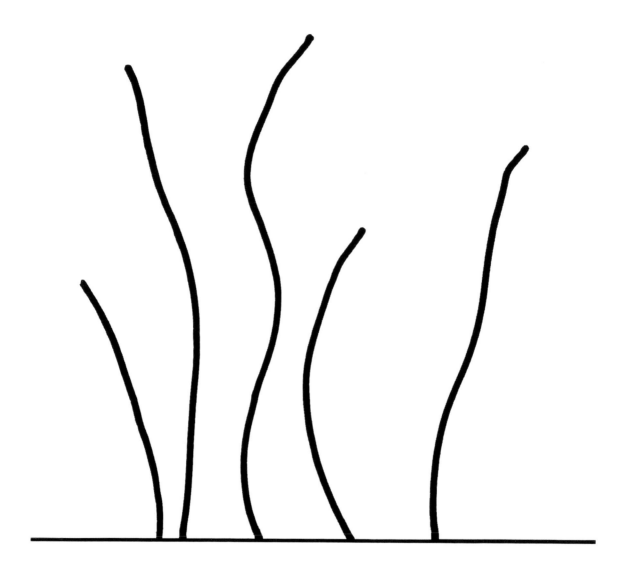

SUN & FLOWER PATTERNS

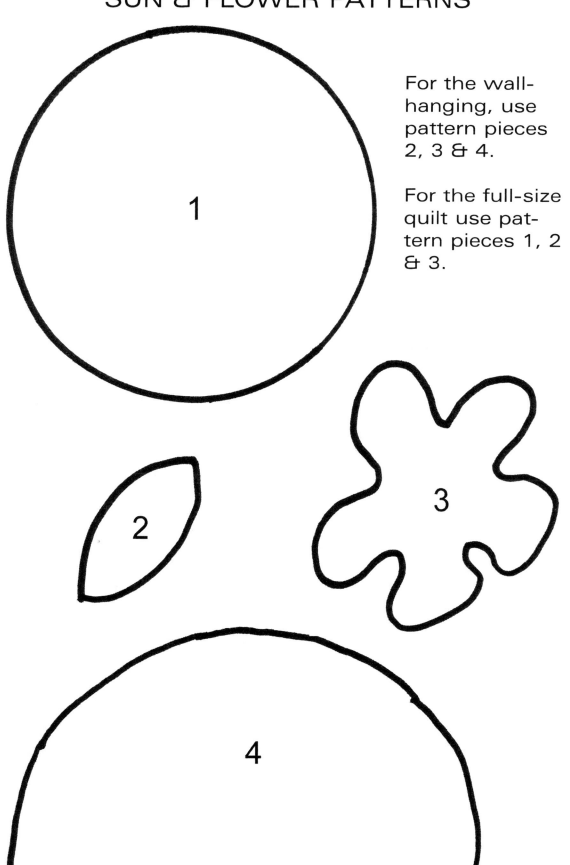

For the wall-hanging, use pattern pieces 2, 3 & 4.

For the full-size quilt use pattern pieces 1, 2 & 3.

INDEX